# Amazing Animal
# Engineers

by Leon Gray

CAPSTONE PRESS
a capstone imprint

Fact Finders are published by Capstone Press,
1710 Roe Crest Drive, North Mankato, Minnesota 56003
www.capstonepub.com

Published in 2016 by Capstone Publishers, Ltd.
Copyright © 2016 Brown Bear Books Ltd.

**Library of Congress Cataloging-in-Publication Data**
Cataloging-in-publication information is on file with the Library of Congress

ISBN: 978-1-4914-6980-4 (hardcover)
ISBN: 978-1-4914-6990-3 (paperback)
ISBN: 978-1-4914-7000-8 (eBook PDF)

**For Brown Bear Books Ltd:**
Text: Leon Gray
Editor: Tim Harris
Picture Researcher: Clare Newman
Designer: Karen Perry
Design Manager: Keith Davis
Production Director: Alastair Gourlay
Editorial Director: Lindsey Lowe
Children's Publisher: Anne O'Daly

**Photo Credits**
Front cover: Shutterstock: Florida Stock
1, J.L. Klein & M. L. Hubert/FLPA; 4, YK/Shutterstock; 5, Gordon Wiltshire/Getty Images; 6b, 2009fotofriends/Shutterstock; 6-7,
Ingo Arndt/Minden Pictures/FLPA; 7tl, Eco Print/Shutterstock; 7tr, Ideas Supermarket/Shutterstock; 9t. David Steele/Shutterstock;
9br Fenghui/Shutterstock; 11tr, Iris Photo1/Shutterstock; 11b, Tierfotoagentur/Alamy; 12, Lehrer/Shutterstock; 13t, Eduard
Kyslynskyy/Shutterstock; 13br, Ratikova/Shutterstock; 14, Steve Shoup/Shutterstock; 14-15b, MRGB/Shutterstock; 15tl, Gary
Yim/Shutterstock; 15tr, Outdoorsman/Shutterstock; 16, J.L. Klein & M. L. Hubert/FLPA; 17cr, Galina Barskaya/Dreamstime; 17b,
Mitsuaki Iwago/Minden Pictures/FLPA; 19cr, Lehakok/Shutterstock; 19b, Flock Holt/Shutterstock; 21tr, Henk Bentlage/
Shutterstock; 21b, Henk Bentlage/Shutterstock; 22b, Milosz-G/Shutterstock; 22-23, Frank Guizou/Hemis/Alamy; 23tr, D.
Kucharski & K. Kucharski/Shutterstock; 23br, David Ashley/Shutterstock; 24, Aleksem Stemmer/Shutterstock; 25cr, Natty PTG/
Shutterstock; 25cr, EB Foto/Shutterstock; 26, Denise Brown/Shutterstock; 27cl, Joe Belanger/Shutterstock; 27b, Vicki Beaver/
Alamy; 28, Pumpkin Pie/Alamy; 29t, Piotr Naskrecki/Minden Pictures/FLPA; 29b, Bruce Coleman/Photoshot.
t=top, c=center, b=bottom, l=left, r=right

All Artworks © Brown Bear Books Ltd
Brown Bear Books has made every attempt to contact the copyright holder.
If you have any information please contact licensing@brownbearbooks.co.uk

Printed in China

# Table of Contents

# Introduction

**Animals build an incredible variety of structures in which to sleep, raise their young, or catch prey. Some animals dig in soil or wood. Others build underwater or attach structures to plants.**

Most birds and many **mammals** build shelters. Female polar bears dig caves in the snow to protect themselves from the coldest weather. Spiders spin webs of very strong **silk** to catch prey. Beavers construct "lodges," which can only be reached by swimming underwater.

Animals use a wide variety of different building materials—grass, twigs, hair, feathers, or mud, for example. Some birds take great care when building. Other animals build very simple shelters that are used for just one night. However, not all structures are built for shelter. Some are built to attract mates or trap prey.

Read on to find out about some of the most creative structures built by some of the most amazing engineers in the animal kingdom.

# Inspired by nature

Humans have copied some of these incredible feats of animal engineering to build their own constructions. When people build giant **dams**, they use the same principles as those used by beavers for millions of years. Mountaineers dig caves in the snow to protect themselves from the cold—just like female polar bears. And people weave cloth in the same way that some birds weave their grass nests.

## COPYCAT

Mountain climbers and hikers often build snow caves for shelter too. The walls of the cave **insulate** the people inside from the cold, polar winds and sub-zero temperatures.

## WOW

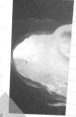

The largest recorded black-tailed prairie dog town extended over 25,000 square miles (65,000 km²) in Texas. Researchers estimated that it contained more than 400 million prairie dogs.

# Guide for readers

Throughout this book, special feature boxes accompany the main text, captioned photographs, and illustrations. COPYCAT boxes highlight some of the ways in which people have been inspired by the animal world. WOW boxes will amaze you with incredible facts and figures about the different animals featured in the book.

# Nest Builders

Animals have been building nests for millions of years. The nests provide shelter from enemies and extreme weather. Nests can be high in trees, on the ground, or in underground burrows. People have copied all these ideas.

## Shelters in trees and underground

Many birds build nests of twigs, leaves, and moss. Weaverbirds spend a long time building neat nests. Other birds build nests that are just a jumble of twigs. Female birds lay eggs in the nests. When the eggs hatch, the parents care for their chicks there. Sometimes, only the female cares for the chicks.

Female chimps build nests in trees. Instead of using the same nest for a long time, though, chimps build a new nest each evening.

Beavers build their homes in ponds. They may make the pond deeper by damming a stream. Other mammals, birds, and insects build nests on the ground. And many animals, including foxes, have their nests in burrows. They dig the burrows themselves or they steal them from other animals.

Beavers build stick homes called lodges in lakes. Part of the lodge is underwater.

BEAVERS CASE STUDY: PAGE 10

Weaverbirds often build nests in the same tree. They are woven together to form a huge community.

**WEAVERBIRDS CASE STUDY:
PAGE 8**

Honeybees live together in a nest, or hive, where they shelter and make food.

**HONEYBEES CASE STUDY:
PAGE 12**

A female chimp and her twins in a nest she has built high in the trees.

# Weaverbirds

Weaverbirds are nest-building experts. These amazing architects build hanging nests in trees using grass stems and other plant fibers. Up to 100 nests can hang from a single tree.

## Jobs for the males

Only the male weavers build the nests. The first step is to tie a blade of grass around a twig to hang the nest. The male keeps a firm hold on the grass with his foot and ties a knot around the twig with his beak.

Then the bird weaves a ring. This ring must be big enough for the bird to pass through but not so big that larger animals can get through. Once the ring is firm, work starts on the roof. The male completes the nest by weaving a long entrance tube. This will stop other animals getting in.

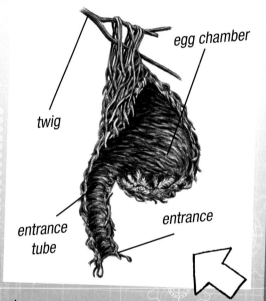

egg chamber

twig

entrance tube

entrance

The weaver attaches a ring of grass strips to a twig, then builds downward. He builds an egg chamber with a long entrance tube to keep out enemies.

The bird collects building materials from a nearby patch of grass. He grips the side of a blade of grass close to the ground and flies straight up, tearing the grass out of the ground as he does so. A weaverbird can use up to 1,000 blades of grass to complete the nest.

Often, groups of weaverbirds build many nests close together in the same tree.

## COPYCAT

A male weaverbird builds its nest in the same way as a person weaves a piece of cloth. The bird threads each blade of grass above and below a series of strips of grass that run at right angles to it. It takes practice to build a good nest.

## Picky females

Females watch the males as they work. They select their mates by their weaving skills. The males show off their nests by hanging upside down from them while calling and fluttering their wings. Eventually, the female makes her choice. A female will not lay eggs in an old nest. If the male has not managed to attract a mate after a few days, he will take his nest apart and start building all over again.

# Beavers

To protect their home, beavers need a pond 3 feet (0.9 m) deep. If the water is not deep enough, these master-builders have a smart solution—they raise the water level by building a dam!

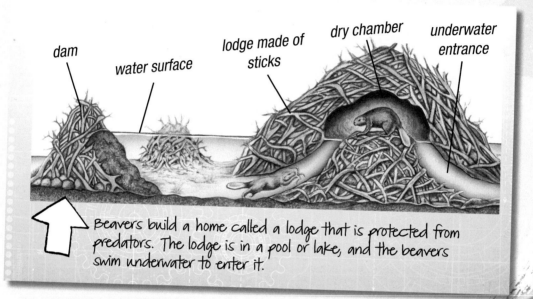

dam

water surface

lodge made of sticks

dry chamber

underwater entrance

Beavers build a home called a lodge that is protected from predators. The lodge is in a pool or lake, and the beavers swim underwater to enter it.

## A dry, warm lodge

Beavers go to amazing lengths to protect themselves from **predators** such as wolves. The way in to the beavers' house, or lodge, can only be reached by swimming underwater. There are usually two chambers inside. The first chamber is for drying off. The animals only go into the second chamber when they are dry. Sometimes it is hard for beavers to find a pond that is deep enough for their lodge. Their clever solution is to build a dam of sticks across a stream. Water piles up behind the dam, and the pond gets deeper.

## Building a dam

A lot of work goes into building a dam. First, the beavers choose a place to build it where the water is not very deep. Then they pick the tree trunks and sticks they will use. They gnaw through trunks with their strong teeth. The beavers push sticks into the mud at the bottom of a stream. The sticks form a **foundation**. When this is in place, the beavers collect thicker logs, bark, rocks, grass, leaves, and mud—and pile them on top of the foundation. A beavers' dam is usually about 6 feet (1.8 m) high.

## COPYCAT

When beavers build a dam, they make it curved, not straight. A curved dam is stronger than a straight one. The Hoover Dam, across the Colorado River, is also curved. Just like beavers, humans use the same idea in their design.

It takes a beaver 20 minutes to gnaw through a tree trunk 6 inches (15 cm) thick.

# Honeybees

Honeybees are social insects. They live in large groups called colonies. A honeybee colony lives in a nest called a hive, which is an engineering wonder of the natural world.

These bees are workers. They are leaving nectar in hexagonal (six-sided) cells.

## Living in a group

There are three main kinds of bees in a colony. The queen rules the hive. Her main job is to lay eggs that will hatch into the next generation of bees. Thousands of male bees, called drones, also live in the hive. During the spring and summer, the drones mate with the queen so she can produce her eggs. The last group in the hive are workers. Their main job is to collect **pollen** and **nectar** from flowers to feed the colony and make honey. The workers feed the drones when they are young and also build, repair, and clean the hive.

A worker bee flies up to a flower to feed on its nectar and collect its pollen.

## Building the hive

Most honeybees build their hives in caves or hollowed-out trees. Some make open hives that hang from the branches of trees. To build the hive, worker bees produce a sticky substance called beeswax. They mold it into perfect hexagonal "cells." All the cells are exactly the same. They fit together to form a very strong structure called a honeycomb.

The bees put the queen's eggs and the young bee **larvae** in some of the cells. Most of the cells are used to store their food—honey and pollen.

## COPYCAT

People have collected honey from the hives of wild bees for thousands of years. The ancient Egyptians were the first people to keep bees. They kept hives in wooden boxes or woven baskets called skeps. Beekeeping is a huge industry today.

13

# Burrowers

A burrow is a tunnel or hole that an animal uses for shelter. Burrows can be anything from a simple hole in the ground to a network of connected chambers and tunnels.

## Burrowing animals

Many different animals live in burrows. They include frogs, snakes, and **invertebrates** such as insects and worms. Some birds, such as puffins and owls, raise their young in burrows instead of nests. Many different kinds of mammals live in burrows. Gophers, groundhogs, moles, and rabbits are examples. Even big mammals such as bears use burrows for shelter in the cold winter months.

Some burrowing animals, such as earthworms and moles, spend almost all their lives underground. Other animals, such as rabbits, spend some time above ground and some time below the surface.

## Burrowing benefits

Living underground has many advantages. It provides a shelter from extreme temperatures and protection from predators. Also, animals can search under the ground for food, such as roots and tubers, grubs, and worms.

These ants are returning to their nest in an underground burrow.

**ANTS CASE STUDY: PAGE 18**

A prairie dog watches for danger at the entrance to its burrow.

**PRAIRIE DOGS CASE STUDY: PAGE 20**

A female polar bear and her cub. Cubs are born in burrows in the snow called dens.

**POLAR BEARS CASE STUDY: PAGE 16**

A mole can dig up to 65 feet (20 m) of tunnels in a day.

# Polar Bears

Polar bears live in the Arctic—one of Earth's most extreme habitats. The weather there is never warm, and for most of the year it is bitterly cold. In fall the days get shorter. By December there is almost no daylight. It is hard for the bears to find food then.

A female polar bear starts to dig a burrow in the snow.

## Building a snow cave

Polar bears mate in April or May. During the short Arctic summer, the weather is a little less cold, and the days are longer. The bears hunt ringed seals in the Arctic Ocean. They need to eat as much as they can before winter sets in. In just four months, a female bear can put on almost 400 pounds (180 kg) in body weight. By October the **pregnant** female starts to dig a den in the snow. She will spend the next eight months in the den without food or water. The female usually builds her den in banks of deep snow along mountain slopes. She scrapes a tunnel into the snow and digs two chambers. One chamber is for sleeping and the other is for giving birth to her cubs.

Cubs are born between November and January. There are usually two cubs, each about 14 inches (35 cm) long. Over the next few months, the mother and her cubs stay in the den to escape the bitter wind and cold of the Arctic winter. The mother feeds the cubs six times a day with rich, fatty milk. The cubs grow quickly, but their mother loses a lot of weight. Eventually, in March or April, the mother and cubs leave their den. The mother leads the cubs out onto the ice to hunt seals.

## COPYCAT

Mountain climbers and hikers often build snow caves for shelter too. The walls of the cave **insulate** the people inside from the cold, polar winds and sub-zero temperatures.

Two bear cubs and their mother have just left the den where the cubs were born.

# Ants

Ants live in social groups called colonies, like bees do. An ant colony has thousands of ants, ruled by a queen. The ants work together to find food, defend the colony, and build a home.

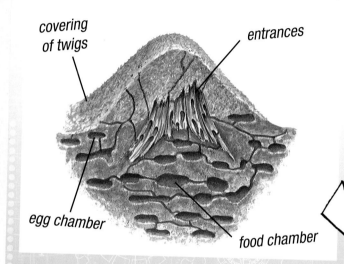

covering of twigs

entrances

egg chamber

food chamber

A queen ant shares her nest with many worker ants. The workers collect food, clean and repair chambers, and move the queen's eggs to special chambers. The eggs grow into grubs, then into adults.

## Protecting the colony

Most ants make their burrows in damp soil. As they dig, the worker ants push the soil out behind them. This leaves a mound of dirt, called an "ant hill," on the surface. The burrow below consists of one or more underground chambers and a system of connected tunnels. At least one of these tunnels will lead to the surface, allowing the ants to leave and search for food. Most burrows have more than one entrance and exit, leaving an escape route if a predator such as a spider or other ants raid the colony.

## Homes in other places

Carpenter ants make their home inside tree trunks and the stems of other large plants. As they chew through the woody fibers, they leave tunnels behind them.

Tropical weaver ants roll leaves into ball-shaped chambers, "sewing" them together with the silky thread that the ant larvae produce. Each worker ant holds a larva in its jaws and uses it like a tube of glue.

In 2009 scientists wrote about an enormous population of ants living along a 3,700-mile (6,000 km) stretch of the coastline of the Mediterranean Sea, in southern Europe. They believe that it is a "supercolony" with billions of ants in millions of burrows.

This ant hill was created as ants dug tunnels and chambers in the soil.

19

# Prairie Dogs

Prairie dogs are rodents that live in burrows beneath the grasslands, or prairies, of North America. Some prairie dogs live in underground "towns." These towns may contain hundreds of family groups called "coteries."

entrance

sleeping chamber

Safe and warm, a prairie dog family sleeps in a chamber under the ground. In winter, prairie dogs may spend the coldest months undergound in a deep sleep called hibernation.

"bed" of grass

## Living in a maze

A family group of prairie dogs usually has an adult male, a few adult females, and their young. Each family lives in a network of tunnels and chambers. The rodents dig all the burrows themselves, using their strong feet. The obvious signs of prairie dog burrows are the raised mounds of loose soil at the surface. The prairie dogs use these mounds as lookout posts to keep watch for predators such as coyotes and snakes. Inside the burrow, there are chambers for sleeping and storing food. Young prairie dogs have their own chambers.

Family members spend a lot of time building and repairing their homes. Their burrows often provide a home for other animals, such as ferrets.

## Safety in numbers

Most prairie dogs defend their family group from neighboring family groups. The black-tailed prairie dog is much friendlier. The coteries of these animals are grouped together in wards. In turn, the wards make up a colony or "town," which may contain hundreds of black-tailed prairie dogs.

# WOW

The largest recorded black-tailed prairie dog town extended over 25,000 square miles (65,000 km²) in Texas. Researchers estimated that it contained more than 400 million prairie dogs.

Five black-tailed prairie dogs stand on a lookout post, watching for danger.

# Trappers

**Predators use various ways to catch their prey. Some rely on speed, while others use camouflage to blend in with their surroundings. A few hunting animals engineer traps to catch their victims.**

## Insect trappers

Many different kinds of insects use traps to catch their prey. Glowworm larvae live in damp caves and spin slimy webs that glow in the dark. The light attracts flying insects, which become trapped in the slime. Ant lion larvae dig funnel-shaped sand pits to trap passing insects.

Some ants that live in trees build tiny platforms made from plant hairs. The ants then cut holes in the platforms and wait underneath. A flying insect may land on one of these platforms to rest. Then the ants climb through the holes and eat their prey.

## Web builders

Web-building spiders spin webs of sticky silk threads. When insects fly into the web, they become trapped, and the spider moves in for the kill.

A spider waits in the middle of its web. If an insect flies into the web it will get stuck.

SPIDERS CASE STUDY: PAGE 24

Ant lions dig sandpits to trap other insects and spiders.

**ANT LIONS CASE STUDY: PAGE 28**

Humpback whales trap fish by blowing rings of bubbles around them.

**HUMPBACK WHALES CASE STUDY: PAGE 26**

These sticky threads are made by glowworms. Insects get stuck to them. The trapped insects are then eaten by the glowworms.

# Spiders

Spiders are deadly predators that spin a web of incredibly strong silk to trap their prey. The largest web that has been measured was 80 feet (24 m) from one side to the other.

The web of an orb web spider is made from silk fibers made inside the spider's body.

## Building the web

The most familiar type of web is called an orb web. You will see these webs in your backyard or local park. A spider starts building an orb web using a single silk thread. This thread forms a bridge between two fixed points, such as the branches of a tree. The spider walks across the bridge, spinning a second silk thread that droops down below the bridge. The spider lowers itself from the middle of this drooping thread, forming a Y-shaped frame. The spider spins more threads to fix the frame in place.

Next, the spider builds "radius threads" from the center to the outer edge of the web. Finally, it spins a sticky thread that spirals in from the outer edge toward the center of the web. The spider sits in the middle of the web, waiting for an insect or bug to fly into its sticky spiral trap.

## Other spider webs

Funnel-web spiders build funnel-shaped webs leading into their underground burrows. Other spiders work together in colonies, building huge silk sheets to trap prey. The net-casting spider is an **ambush** predator. It builds a small, sticky web between its legs and throws the "net" over passing prey to trap it.

## COPYCAT

Spider silk seems fragile, but it is very strong. Ounce for ounce, the silk is five times stronger than steel. Human engineers are looking at ways to make artificial spider silk for their own projects.

If an insect enters a funnel-web spider's silky funnel, the spider runs out to kill it.

# Humpback Whales

Humpback whales use a clever trick to trap prey such as fish. They use their breath to blow a net of bubbles, trapping great numbers of fish near the surface of the water. The whales then swim up to the surface to feast on the fish.

Several humpbacks rise to the surface of the water after making a "bubble net."

## Filter feeders

Humpbacks are **baleen** whales. These giant sea mammals usually feed on tiny ocean creatures called krill and plankton. Humpbacks have large baleen plates hanging inside their mouths. Baleen is similar to the material that makes human hair and nails. The whales swim with their mouths wide open. The baleen plates act like sieves to collect huge quantities of krill and plankton from the water.

## COPYCAT

Fishers on big ships in the ocean use a net called a purse seine to catch fish in a similar way to humpback whales. Purse seine nets draw large numbers of fish into a small area, and the fishers can then scoop the fish out of the water.

## Bubble nets

Humpback whales live in all the world's great oceans. In the winter, they breed in the warm waters near the **equator**. The whales then **migrate** to summer feeding grounds near the poles. The humpbacks are very hungry after the long migration. They use bubble netting to collect fish in great numbers.

The whales work in teams of up to 12. They swim around shoals of fish such as herrings, mackerels, and salmon. When they have trapped the fish, all the humpbacks help themselves to their share of the food.

A humpback whale opens its mouth wide. Its baleen plates hang from its upper jaw.

# Ant Lions

Ant lions are the larvae of winged insects that look like damselflies. Although ant lion larvae are only small, they are fierce predators. They make sand pit traps to catch their prey.

These little pits have been made by ant lions. Small insects get stuck in the pits.

## Living in the sand

Adult ant lions live in many different parts of the world. They are very common in dry, sandy **habitats**. The adult female ant lions lay their eggs in the sand, and the young hatch a few days later. The larvae have round bodies, with six short legs and hollow, pincerlike jaws. They use their jaws to kill and eat other small insects.

An adult ant lion has wings and looks very different from a larva, or young ant lion.

Ant lions are often called doodlebugs because they leave trails in the sand as they look for a suitable spot to build their traps. These trails look like "doodles" in the sand.

## Death trap

Ant lions have a clever way of catching their prey. They use their short legs to dig funnel-shaped pits in the sand about 2 inches (5 cm) deep. Then they lie in wait at the bottom. Spiders and small insects such as ants slip on the loose sand and fall into the trap. The ant lion quickly moves in and injects its prey with **venom** to **paralyze** it. The ant lion then uses its hollow jaws like a straw to suck the juices from its victim's lifeless body.

# Glossary

**ambush** a surprise attack by a predator lying in wait for its prey

**baleen** bristly material inside a whale's mouth that filters tiny creatures from the ocean

**burrows** holes or tunnels in the ground that an animal uses for shelter

**camouflage** the way some animals blend in with their surroundings to avoid being seen

**colonies** groups of animals, such as ants, that live together

**dams** barriers that stop the flow of water in a river or stream

**equator** an imaginary horizontal line around the center of the Earth

**foundation** the underlying building blocks of a structure such as a beaver's lodge or a building

**habitats** the natural homes of animals or plants

**insulate** to keep something warm

**invertebrates** animals without backbones, such as insects

**larvae** the maggotlike forms of young insects

**mammals** animals with warm blood and fur; female mammals produce milk to feed their young

**migrate** to move from one habitat to another when the seasons change

**nectar** a sweet liquid produced by many plants

**paralyze** to make something unable to move

**pollen** fine dust made by flowers

**predators** animals that hunt and eat other animals

**pregnant** when a female animal carries developing offspring inside her body

**silk** a strong, fine fiber produced by spiders and many insects

**venom** a poisonous chemical produced by animals such as spiders and snakes

# Read more

**Bradley, Timothy.** *Animal Architects* (Time for Kids). Huntington Beach, CA: Teacher Created Materials Publishing, 2012.

**Kalman, Bobbie.** *Baby Animals in Grassland Habitats* (Habitats of Baby Animals). New York: Crabtree, 2014.

**Rustad, Martha.** *Insects* (Little Scientist). North Mankato, MN: Capstone, 2014.

**Sharma, Garima.** *Nature's Architects* (Work Squad). New Delhi, India: TERI, 2011.

**Spilsbury, Richard.** *Look Inside a Burrow* (Young Explorer). North Mankato, MN: Capstone, 2013.

**Taylor, Saranne.** *Animal Homes* (Young Architect). New York: Crabtree, 2014.

# Internet Sites

FactHound offers a safe, fun way to find Internet sites related to this book. All of the sites on FactHound have been researched by our staff.

Here's all you do:

Visit www.facthound.com

Type in this code: 9781491469804

 Check out projects, games and lots more at
**www.capstonekids.com**

# Index